Cooking School

MEDITERRANEAN

Cooking School

MEDITERRANEAN

Bring the flavours of the Mediterranean to life in your own kitchen!

This edition published in 2011
LOVE FOOD is an imprint of Parragon Books Ltd

Parragon
Queen Street House
4 Queen Street
Bath BA1 1HE, UK

www.parragon.com

ISBN: 978-1-4454-7028-3

Printed in China

Internal design by Pink Creative

Notes for the Reader

This book uses both metric and imperial measurements. Follow the same units of measurement throughout; do not mix metric and imperial. All spoon measurements are level: teaspoons are assumed to be 5 ml, and tablespoons are assumed to be 15 ml. Unless otherwise stated, milk is assumed to be full fat, eggs and individual vegetables are medium, and pepper is freshly ground black pepper.

The times given are an approximate guide only. Preparation times differ according to the techniques used by different people and the cooking times may also vary from those given. Optional ingredients, variations or serving suggestions have not been included in the calculations.

Recipes using raw or very lightly cooked eggs should be avoided by infants, the elderly, pregnant women, convalescents and anyone suffering from an illness. Pregnant and breastfeeding women are advised to avoid eating peanuts and peanut products. Sufferers from nut allergies should be aware that some of the ready-made ingredients used in the recipes in this book may contain nuts. Always check the packaging before use.

Contents

Introduction

Year-round sunshine, an outstanding coastline and a rich history make the Mediterranean the most widely visited region in the world, with a correspondingly acclaimed cuisine. It is a vast area, stretching from Gibraltar at the western end, through Spain, southern France and Italy, across to Slovenia and down the Dalmatian coast to Albania and Greece, on to Turkey and the Middle East, and back again along the North African coast to Morocco.

It is a region of brilliant colours, not only from the sky and the sea, but from the profusion of vegetables and fruit in the markets – gleaming peppers and tomatoes, inky aubergines and olives, cool green leaves, musky melons and peaches, plump purple figs, scarlet cherries and much more. There are huge vans festooned with richly coloured sausages and cured meats, dazzling displays of shining silvery fish – spanking fresh and smelling sweetly of the sea – and stalls piled high with every imaginable type of cheese from minuscule goat's cheeses to massive wheels of Parmesan.

National and Regional Variations

Though Mediterranean countries share a coastline and a similar climate, to speak of the cuisine as a single one is misleading. Within it is a cornucopia of dishes with distinct national and regional variations – from hearty Spanish bean and sausage stews, French fish soups and Italian pasta dishes to the cool yogurt soups of the Balkans, honeyed Greek pastries and salty sheep's cheese, Middle-Eastern falafel, creamy hummus and flatbreads, and the fragrant tagines and couscous of North Africa.

The differences are apparent in the use of spices and herbs. North African cooks use complex spice blends such as 'ras el hanout' from Morocco or the heady Tunisian five-spice mix 'qalat daqqa'. In the Middle East, cinnamon, allspice and cumin predominate, as do leafy green herbs, such as parsley and mint. In Italy, France and Spain fewer spices are used, and cooks rely more on robust herbs such as rosemary, thyme and marjoram.

Cooking Equipment

You are likely to have most of the pots and pans necessary for producing authentic Mediterranean-style dishes. There are, however, a few special items that will do the job more effectively.

BRAISING PAN

With the lid in place, this is the pan to use for dishes, such as braised meats or moules marinières, that need a minimum of liquid. Without the lid, the rounded, slightly flared sides make it the ideal pan for dishes that need stirring, such as risotto, paella and polenta. The large surface area encourages evaporation so the pan is also good for reducing and thickening liquids intended for a sauce.

PASTA POT

A large pot is essential not only for pasta but also for stock-making and hearty Mediterranean soups, such as harira and bouillabaisse. A perforated insert is handy for lifting out cooked pasta, leaving the liquid behind – far safer than carrying a heavy pot from hob to sink.

PERFORATED PIZZA PAN

A perforated metal pizza pan allows heat and air to reach the centre of the dough, creating a crisper crust than is possible with a solid baking sheet.

PIZZA STONE

For the very best results, use an unglazed ceramic pizza stone. Preheated in a very hot oven, the stone draws moisture from the dough, producing a top-notch crisp, yet chewy, crust.

RECTANGULAR CERAMIC GRATIN DISH

A large gratin dish deep enough for several layers of food is perfect for lasagne and moussaka. A proper gratin dish has a thick ridge round the top for easy lifting, and gently outward-sloping sides that increase the surface area for browning the topping.

SAUTÉ PAN WITH LID

A sauté pan has a wide diameter and high straight sides that allow quick browning of bulky items, such as chicken quarters and chops, or large amounts of vegetables as in ratatouille. The high sides prevent splattering and spilling as the food is turned. Once it is evenly browned and the lid is in place, the food can cook at a more leisurely pace without burning or drying out.

TAGINE

Named after the North African dish of the same name, a tagine is a uniquely shaped thick pot with a tall conical lid and a wide shallow base. Very little liquid is needed as the lid provides a large cool surface on which steam condenses and drips onto the food below, without diluting the flavour. Traditionally made of earthenware for use over an open fire, the modern tagine has a cast-iron base that can be used on any type of hob.

Essential Ingredients

Delicatessens and supermarkets offer an ever-increasing range of Mediterranean ingredients, and it is sometimes difficult to decide what to choose. The following list gives you all-important know-how.

BALSAMIC VINEGAR

A speciality from Modena in northern Italy, balsamic vinegar is used as a condiment rather than a salad dressing component. The quality and price vary enormously. 'Aged' balsamic vinegar is the most expensive, but a little goes a long way. This is the one to use for a thick syrupy glaze or for sprinkling over salads. For everyday use, choose a medium-priced vinegar, preferably labelled 'di Modena'. Cheap balsamic vinegar is often 'enhanced' with caramel colouring and is not worth buying.

BULGAR WHEAT

This is wheat grain that has been part-cooked, dried and cracked. The grain is then ready for cooking in a seasoned liquid. Once rinsed, uncooked grains readily absorb liquids, so can simply be left to stand in tomato juice or lemon juice until softened. Bulgar wheat is used in tabbouleh, a Middle-Eastern salad, and for stuffing courgettes, peppers and other vegetables.

COUSCOUS

This is the name of the grain and the dish itself. Couscous is made from durum wheat semolina. It is used throughout North Africa and the Middle East and comes in various grades, ranging from fine grains to those the size of small pearls. Couscous sold in supermarkets is generally fine-grained and precooked, and needs only to be steamed or left to stand in very hot water. Use 3 parts couscous to 5 parts water, and leave to stand for at least 30 minutes before fluffing with a fork.

OLIVE OIL

Cold-pressed extra virgin olive oil, preferably estate-bottled, is essential for salad dressings, anointing vegetables and grilled fish, and for bread-dipping. It has a wonderful peppery, grassy flavour. It is rarely used for cooking as it burns too easily. Always buy extra virgin oil in dark glass bottles or cans, and store in a cool place; light and heat speed up deterioration.
Virgin olive oil, or supermarket-grade oil, has a milder flavour and is the next best grade to cold-pressed extra virgin oil. It can be used for cooking all kinds of Mediterranean food, and for making mayonnaise and aïoli.

PASTA

Dried pasta is usually a better choice than shop-bought fresh pasta, which is often thick and rubbery. It will also keep indefinitely if stored in a dry place.

There are two basic types: flour-and-water pasta made with hard durum wheat flour (semolina) and water, and egg pasta made with plain flour and eggs. Both come in an extraordinary number of shapes, each lending itself to a particular type of sauce. Long round or flat pasta is best for tomato- or oil-based sauces that cling to the pasta. Tubes and shapes are ideal for trapping chunkier sauces in their crevices. Egg pasta is more absorbent and is best with butter- or cream-based sauces.

POLENTA

A staple food in northern Italy, polenta is made from coarsely ground cornmeal, mixed with water and cooked until thickened. Depending on the amount of water added, it is served wet in the same way as mashed potatoes, often mixed with cheese, or cooled until firm and cut into shapes before grilling or frying until crisp. Ordinary polenta has a better flavour and texture than 'quick-cook' brands.

PULSES

Beans, lentils and chickpeas are sold dried or in cans. With the exception of lentils, dried pulses need lengthy soaking but they have a better flavour and texture than canned pulses. Make sure they are well within the 'use-by' date; stale pulses need a much longer cooking time.

Dried beans and chickpeas are particularly popular in the Middle East, where they are mashed and fried to make irresistible falafel.

RISOTTO RICE

This is a short-grain white rice from northern Italy. It releases starch when constantly stirred in hot liquid and this creates the characteristic creamy texture of the dish after which it is named. The most well-known variety is arborio, but the very best varieties are vialone nano and carnaroli.

Tips and Techniques

Mediterranean-style cooking is wonderfully straightforward, but a few simple tricks of the trade are well worth mastering.

Bread and pizza dough

- Yeast thrives in warm surroundings, so do make sure the ingredients and equipment are warm before you begin.
- Always sift the flour first to remove lumps and incorporate air. Add the specified amount of salt when sifting to distribute it evenly.
- For lukewarm water, use 1 part boiling water to 2 parts cold water.
- The amount of liquid needed may vary from that specified in the recipe, depending on the type of flour and the amount of moisture in the air. Always keep back a little of the flour and water so you can adjust the consistency as necessary.
- Knead the dough for at least 10 minutes until silky smooth and springy.
- Put the kneaded dough in a deep, lightly oiled bowl to rise. The oil allows the dough to rise smoothly without sticking to the sides of the bowl.
- Bake pizza at the highest possible temperature in the top of the oven. Use a pizza stone or perforated pizza pan for the best results.

Pasta

- Pasta must be cooked in plenty of water so that it can move freely in the pan. Use a pasta pot or very large saucepan, allowing 1 litre/1¾ pints of water for every 100 g/3½ oz of pasta.
- There is no need to add olive oil if you use the correct amount of water. Bring the water to a fast boil, then add salt and pasta, stirring to prevent sticking.
- Cover the pan until the water boils again, then remove the lid and cook according to the packet instructions.
- Always cook the sauce before the pasta. The sauce can usually be kept waiting, but if you leave cooked pasta to stand, it will start to become sticky.

Polenta

- For a medium consistency, use 1 part polenta to 5 parts water. For a soft consistency use 1 part polenta to 7 parts water.
- Bring the water to the boil in a large saucepan, add salt, then reduce the heat to a medium simmer. Using a long-handled wooden spoon, stir with one hand, and add the polenta in a steady stream with the other, sifting it through your fingers like sand.
- Cook, stirring, for up to 20 minutes, or until the polenta comes away from the sides of the pan. If serving wet, simply spoon into a serving bowl, otherwise pour into a wide shallow pan and smooth the top with a wet palette knife.
- Allow to set before cutting into shapes for frying or grilling.

Risotto

- Do not wash risotto rice – the starch from the grains is an essential part of the dish.
- Use a wide saucepan or braising pan, or a high-sided frying pan, suitable for the amount of rice you intend to cook. Remember that rice will expand to three times its volume.
- Make sure the stock is hot before you stir it into the rice. Keep the stock simmering in a small saucepan. Add a ladleful at a time, and stir until the liquid is absorbed before adding the next ladleful.
- Once cooked, the grains should be creamy, but still firm to the bite.

Soups and Starters

Soups are a vital part of Mediterranean life and each country has its specialities. They vary in consistency from hearty meal-in-a-bowl soups, such as densely mellow Italian Minestrone or Classic Lamb, Chickpea and Lentil Soup from Morocco, to clean-tasting chilled soups that perk up the appetite on a sweltering day – Spanish Gazpacho, for example.

With its extensive coastline, the Mediterranean also boasts plenty of fish-based soups, traditionally made from the remains of the fishermen's catch. Intensely garlicky and packed with seafood and delicious white-fleshed fish, Bouillabaisse is a French classic, albeit with many local variations. Another is Greek Fisherman's Soup or 'kakavia', the name of the pot in which it was traditionally cooked.

Equally important throughout the Mediterranean is the very civilized custom of serving a spread of small tasty dishes with pre-meal drinks, or to enjoy as a starter while waiting for the rest of the meal.

In Italy you'll find craggy pieces of toasted bruschetta with delicious toppings, ranging from chicken livers to basil-scented diced tomatoes and onion. In Spain, a tapas selection is likely to include wedges of tortilla, spicy fried potatoes or tiny meatballs in a tasty sauce. In the Middle East, you'll find Hummus and relatively substantial dishes, such as crisp fried Falafel or juicy kebabs. No matter how simple or elaborate, these tasty appetizers always hit the spot.

Gazpacho

SERVES 4

1 red pepper, cored, deseeded and
    chopped

1 kg/2 lb 4 oz ripe tomatoes, peeled,
    deseeded and chopped

2 tbsp very finely chopped onion

3 garlic cloves, crushed

1 cucumber, peeled and chopped

100 g/3½ oz stale bread, crumbled

3 tbsp red wine vinegar or sherry
    vinegar

3½ tbsp olive oil, plus extra for drizzling

200 g/7 oz ice cubes (optional)

salt and pepper

1. Set aside a handful of the red pepper, a handful of the tomatoes and half the
   chopped onion in the refrigerator. Put the rest in a food processor with the garlic
   and cucumber and purée until smooth. Add the bread, vinegar and oil and whizz
   again. Season to taste with salt and pepper. If the soup is too thick, add the ice,
   then place in the refrigerator for 2 hours.

2. When ready to serve, check the vinegar and seasoning and ladle into bowls.
   Scatter over the reserved red pepper, tomatoes and onions, then drizzle over a
   swirl of olive oil. Serve.

Minestrone

SERVES 4

2 tbsp olive oil

2 garlic cloves, chopped

2 red onions, chopped

75 g/2¾ oz Parma ham, sliced

1 red pepper, deseeded and chopped

1 orange pepper, deseeded and chopped

400 g/14 oz canned chopped tomatoes

1 litre/1¾ pints vegetable stock

1 celery stick, chopped

400 g/14 oz canned borlotti beans, drained

100 g/3½ oz green leafy cabbage, shredded

75 g/2¾ oz frozen peas, thawed

1 tbsp chopped fresh parsley

75 g/2¾ oz dried vermicelli

salt and pepper

freshly grated Parmesan cheese, to garnish

1. Heat the oil in a large saucepan. Add the garlic, onions and ham and cook over a medium heat, stirring, for 3 minutes until slightly soft. Add the red pepper, orange pepper and tomatoes and cook for a further 2 minutes, stirring.

2. Stir in the stock, then add the celery. Add the beans along with the cabbage, peas and parsley. Season to taste with salt and pepper. Bring to the boil, then reduce the heat and simmer for 30 minutes.

3. Add the vermicelli to the pan. Cook for a further 4–5 minutes, or according to the instructions on the packet. Remove from the heat and ladle into warmed serving bowls. Garnish with freshly grated Parmesan cheese and serve immediately.

Classic Lamb, Chickpea and Lentil Soup

SERVES 4

2–3 tbsp olive oil or argan oil

2 onions, chopped

2 celery sticks, diced

2 small carrots, peeled and diced

2–3 garlic cloves, peeled and lightly crushed but kept whole

1 tbsp cumin seeds

450 g/1 lb lean lamb, cut into bite-sized cubes

2–3 tsp ground turmeric

2 tsp paprika

2 tsp ground cinnamon

2 tsp granulated sugar

2 bay leaves

2 tbsp tomato purée

1 litre/1¾ pints lamb stock or chicken stock

400 g/14 oz canned chopped tomatoes, drained

400 g/14 oz canned chickpeas, drained and rinsed

100 g/3½ oz brown lentils or green lentils, thoroughly rinsed

1 small bunch of fresh flat-leaf parsley, roughly chopped

1 small bunch of fresh coriander, roughly chopped

salt and pepper

1 lemon, cut into quarters, to serve

1. Heat the oil in a deep, heavy-based saucepan, add the onions, celery and carrots and cook over a medium heat for 2–3 minutes, stirring frequently, until the onions begin to colour.

2. Add the garlic, cumin seeds and lamb and cook, stirring, until the lamb is lightly browned all over. Add the spices, sugar and bay leaves and stir in the tomato purée. Pour in the stock and bring to the boil. Reduce the heat, cover and simmer for 1 hour, or until the meat is tender.

3. Add the tomatoes, chickpeas and lentils and simmer gently for a further 30 minutes, or until the lentils are soft and the soup is almost as thick as a stew. Discard the bay leaves. Season to taste with salt and pepper and toss in most of the parsley and coriander.

4. Garnish with the remaining parsley and coriander and serve the soup piping hot with lemon wedges for squeezing over.

Bouillabaisse

SERVES 8

1 kg/2 lb 4 oz selection of at least
    4 different firm white fish fillets, such
    as red mullet, snapper, sea bass, eel
    or monkfish, scaled and cleaned,
    but not skinned
100 ml/3½ fl oz olive oil
2 onions, finely chopped
1 fennel bulb, finely chopped
4 garlic cloves, crushed
1.2 kg/2 lb 6 oz canned chopped plum
    tomatoes
1.5 litres/2¾ pints fish stock

pinch of saffron strands
grated zest of 1 orange
bouquet garni of 2 sprigs thyme,
    2 sprigs parsley and 2 bay leaves,
    tied together with string
500 g/1 lb 2 oz mussels, cleaned
500 g/1 lb 2 oz cooked prawns, shell on
salt and pepper
crusty baguette and rouille,
    to serve

1. Carefully pin-bone the fish, then cut the fillets into bite-sized pieces.

2. Heat the oil in a very large frying pan or wide saucepan with a lid, add the onions
    and fennel and gently fry for about 15 minutes until soft. Add the garlic and fry
    for 2 minutes, then add the tomatoes and simmer for 2 minutes. Add the stock,
    saffron, orange zest and bouquet garni and bring to the boil. Simmer, uncovered,
    for 15 minutes.

3. Add the fish pieces, mussels and prawns and cover the pan. Simmer for a further
    5–10 minutes until the mussels have opened. Discard any that remain closed.
    Check the seasoning.

4. Serve with some crusty baguette and rouille.

Fisherman's Soup

SERVES 6

900 g/2 lb fillets of mixed white fish and shellfish, such as cod, flounder, halibut, monkfish, sea bass, whiting and peeled prawns
150 ml/5 fl oz olive oil
2 large onions, sliced
2 celery sticks, thinly sliced
2 garlic cloves, chopped
150 ml/5 fl oz white wine

4 canned tomatoes, chopped
pared rind of 1 orange
1 tsp chopped fresh thyme
2 tbsp chopped fresh parsley
2 bay leaves
salt and pepper
lemon wedges, to serve
croûtons and sprigs of fresh thyme, to garnish

1. Cut the fish into fairly large, thick serving portions, discarding any skin.

2. Heat the oil in a large saucepan, add the onion, celery and garlic and fry for 5 minutes until soft.

3. Add the fish and prawns to the pan then add the wine, tomatoes, orange rind, thyme, parsley, bay leaves, salt and pepper and enough cold water to cover. Bring to the boil, then simmer, uncovered, for 15 minutes.

4. Serve the soup hot, with lemon wedges, and garnished with croûtons and thyme.

Bruschetta with Tomato, Red Onion and Basil Salsa

SERVES 6

1 large baguette or focaccia loaf

2 tbsp basil oil

2 red onions

10 g/¼ oz basil leaves (green or purple)

10 plum tomatoes, peeled, deseeded and diced

juice of 2 lemons

salt and pepper

1. Preheat the oven to 230°C/450°F/Gas Mark 8.

2. Slice open the baguette. Place on a baking sheet, brush with some of the oil, place in the oven and toast until golden.

3. Chop the onions and basil and combine with the tomatoes, lemon juice and the remaining oil. Add salt and pepper to taste. Spoon the salsa over each slice of toasted bread and serve.

Tomato and Potato Tortilla

SERVES 6

1 kg/2 lb 4 oz potatoes, peeled and cut into small cubes

2 tbsp olive oil

1 bunch spring onions, chopped

115 g/4 oz cherry tomatoes

6 eggs

3 tbsp water

2 tbsp chopped fresh parsley

salt and pepper

1. Bring a saucepan of lightly salted water to the boil, add the potatoes and cook for 8–10 minutes, or until tender. Drain and reserve until required.

2. Preheat the grill to medium. Heat the oil in a large frying pan. Add the spring onions and fry until just soft. Add the potatoes and fry for 3–4 minutes until coated with oil and hot. Smooth the top and scatter over the tomatoes.

3. Mix the eggs, water, parsley and salt and pepper together in a bowl, then pour into the pan. Cook over a very gentle heat for 10–15 minutes until the tortilla is fairly set.

4. Place the pan under the preheated grill and cook until the top is brown and set. Leave to cool for 10–15 minutes before sliding out of the pan on to a chopping board. Cut into wedges and serve immediately.

Falafel

SERVES 4

225 g/8 oz dried chickpeas

1 large onion, finely chopped

1 garlic clove, crushed

2 tbsp chopped fresh parsley,
   plus extra sprigs to garnish

2 tsp ground cumin

2 tsp ground coriander

½ tsp baking powder

cayenne pepper

salt

oil, for deep-frying

TO SERVE

hummus

tomato wedges

pitta bread

1. Soak the chickpeas overnight in enough cold water to cover them and allow room
    for expansion. Drain, then place in a saucepan, cover with fresh water and bring to
    the boil. Reduce the heat and simmer for 1 hour, or until tender. Drain.

2. Place the chickpeas in a food processor and blend to make a coarse paste. Add
    the onion, garlic, parsley, cumin, coriander and baking powder, and cayenne
    pepper and salt to taste. Blend again to mix thoroughly.

3. Cover and leave to rest for 30 minutes, then shape into 8 balls. Leave to rest
    for a further 30 minutes. Heat the oil in a wok or large saucepan to 180–190°C/
    350–375°F, or until a cube of bread browns in 30 seconds. Gently drop in the balls
    and cook until golden brown. Remove from the oil and drain on a plate lined with
    kitchen paper.

4. Serve hot or at room temperature with hummus, tomato wedges and pitta bread.
    Garnish with parsley sprigs.

Shish Kebabs

SERVES 4–6 AS PART OF A MEZE

500 g/1 lb 2 oz boneless leg or neck of
    lamb with a small amount of fat,
    cut into 2-cm/¾-inch cubes

2 green peppers, halved, deseeded and
    cut into 2-cm/¾-inch pieces

1 onion, quartered and separated
    into layers

2 cherry tomatoes per skewer

TO SERVE

lemon wedges

Cucumber and Mint Yogurt
(see page 78)

MARINADE

2 tbsp milk

2 tbsp olive oil, plus extra for brushing

1 large onion, grated

1 tbsp tomato purée

½ tsp ground cumin

coarse sea salt and pepper

1. To make the marinade, put all the ingredients in a bowl and stir until the tomato
   purée is evenly dispersed. Add the lamb cubes and use your hands to coat well
   with the marinade. Cover and leave to marinate in the refrigerator for 2 hours. If
   you are using wooden skewers, soak them in cold water for at least 1 hour.

2. Heat a ridged, cast-iron griddle pan over a very high heat or preheat the grill to its
   highest setting. Lightly brush presoaked wooden or long, flat metal skewers with
   oil, then thread an equal quantity of the lamb cubes onto each one, occasionally
   interspersing with green pepper pieces, onion layers and tomatoes. Sprinkle
   with salt.

3. Brush the griddle pan or grill rack with oil. Add the kebabs and cook, turning
   frequently and basting with the remaining marinade, for 8–10 minutes, or until the
   lamb and peppers are charred on the edges. Cut one lamb cube open to check
   that the meat is cooked to your liking.

4. Using a folded cloth to protect your fingers, hold the top of each skewer and use a
   fork to push the ingredients onto a serving platter. Serve immediately with lemon
   wedges and Cucumber and Mint Yogurt.

Peppered Pork Bruschetta

SERVES 4–6

350 g/12 oz pork fillet, cut crossways
   into 12 slices
1 small sourdough loaf
5 tbsp olive oil, plus extra for brushing
   the bread
2 tomatoes, sliced
2 large gherkins, diagonally sliced

MARINADE
1 tsp black peppercorns
1 tsp fennel seeds
1 tsp paprika
½ tsp sea salt flakes
2 garlic cloves, chopped
grated zest of ½ lemon
1 tbsp olive oil

1. Place the pork slices between two sheets of clingfilm and flatten with a mallet
    until thin.

2. Grind the marinade ingredients to a paste, using a mortar and pestle. Rub the
    paste into the meat and leave to marinate for 30 minutes at room temperature or
    overnight in the refrigerator. Allow to come to room temperature before cooking.

3. Slice into six 1-cm/½-inch slices, using the wider part of the loaf. Lightly toast
    on both sides. Brush one side with oil and cut each slice in half. Set aside and
    keep warm.

4. Heat a large frying pan over a medium–high heat. Pour in the oil, add the pork and
    fry, in batches if necessary, for 1 minute on each side.

5. Place a tomato slice on each piece of toast, and top with the pork. Finish with a
    gherkin slice and serve warm or at room temperature.

Spanish Mountain Ham Croquettes

MAKES 8

4 tbsp Spanish olive oil

1 small onion, finely chopped

1 garlic clove, crushed

4 tbsp plain flour

200 ml/7 fl oz milk

200 g/7 oz serrano ham or cooked ham, in one piece, finely diced

pinch of hot or sweet smoked Spanish paprika

1 egg

55 g/2 oz day-old white breadcrumbs

sunflower oil, for deep-frying

salt

aïoli, to serve

1. Heat the olive oil in a saucepan, add the onion and cook over a medium heat, stirring occasionally, for 5 minutes, or until soft but not brown. Add the garlic and cook, stirring, for 30 seconds. Stir in the flour and cook over a low heat, stirring constantly, for 1 minute without the mixture colouring.

2. Remove the saucepan from the heat and gradually stir in the milk to form a smooth sauce. Return to the heat and slowly bring to the boil, stirring constantly, until the sauce boils and thickens. Remove the saucepan from the heat, stir in the ham and paprika and season to taste with salt. Spread the mixture in a shallow dish and leave to cool, then cover and chill in the refrigerator for at least 2 hours or overnight.

3. When the mixture has chilled, break the egg onto a plate and beat lightly. Spread the breadcrumbs on a separate plate. Using wet hands, form the ham mixture into eight even-sized pieces and form each piece into a cylindrical shape. Dip the croquettes, one at a time, into the beaten egg, then roll in the breadcrumbs to coat. Put on a plate and chill in the refrigerator for at least 1 hour.

4. Heat enough sunflower oil for deep-frying in a deep-fat fryer to 180–190°C/350–375°F, or until a cube of bread browns in 30 seconds. Add the croquettes, in batches to avoid overcrowding, and cook for 5 minutes, or until golden brown and crisp. Remove with a slotted spoon or draining basket and drain on kitchen paper. Keep hot in a warm oven while you cook the remaining croquettes. Serve hot with aïoli.

Grilled Chicken Wings with Tahini Sauce

SERVES 4–6

8 chicken wings, halved
warmed pitta bread, to serve

MARINADE
3 tbsp olive oil
2 tsp smoked Spanish paprika
1 tsp cumin seeds, crushed
½ tsp dried oregano
2 large garlic cloves, crushed
salt and pepper

TAHINI SAUCE
1 large garlic clove, crushed
¼ tsp salt
125 ml/4 fl oz tahini, well stirred
juice of 1½ lemons
6–8 tbsp water

1. Put the chicken wings in a shallow dish. Combine the marinade ingredients and rub into the chicken. Cover and leave to marinate in the refrigerator for 2–24 hours. Allow to come to room temperature before cooking.

2. To make the sauce, crush the garlic and salt to a paste, using a mortar and pestle. Transfer to a blender with the tahini and lemon juice. Process until smooth, adding enough water to make a creamy sauce. Pour into a serving bowl and set aside.

3. Preheat the grill. Place the wings on a rack in a foil-lined grill pan, and brush with the oily marinade remaining in the dish. Position the pan about 15 cm/6 inches from the heat source and grill for 12–15 minutes, turning once, until golden and the flesh is no longer pink. Tip into a serving bowl and pour over the pan juices.

4. Serve with the tahini sauce and fingers of pitta bread.

Tuna and Olive Empanadillas

MAKES ABOUT 32

175 g/6 oz canned tuna in olive oil

1 small onion, finely chopped

1 garlic clove, finely chopped

50 g/1¾ oz pimiento-stuffed Spanish olives, finely chopped

25 g/1 oz pine kernels

500 g/1 lb 2 oz ready-made puff pastry, thawed if frozen

salt and pepper

plain flour, for dusting

beaten egg, to glaze

1. Drain the tuna, reserving the oil, put in a large bowl and set aside.

2. Heat 1 tablespoon of the reserved oil from the tuna in a large frying pan, add the onion and cook over a medium heat, stirring occasionally, for 5 minutes, or until soft but not brown. Add the garlic and cook, stirring, for 30 seconds until soft.

3. Mash the tuna with a fork, then add the onion mixture, olives and pine kernels and mix together well. Season to taste with salt and pepper.

4. Preheat the oven to 200°C/400°F/Gas Mark 6. Dampen several large baking sheets. Thinly roll out the pastry on a lightly floured work surface. Using a plain, 8-cm/3¼-inch round cutter, cut out 32 rounds, re-rolling the trimmings as necessary. Using a teaspoon, put an equal, small amount of the tuna mixture in the centre of each pastry round. Dampen the edges of the pastry with a little water and fold one half over the other to form a crescent and enclose the filling. Pinch the edges together with your fingers to seal, then press with the tines of a fork to seal further. Transfer to the prepared baking sheets.

5. With the tip of a sharp knife, make a small slit in the top of each pastry and brush with beaten egg. Place in the preheated oven and bake for 15 minutes, or until risen and golden brown. Serve warm.

Baked Scallops

SERVES 6

700 g/1 lb 9 oz shelled scallops, chopped
2 onions, finely chopped
2 garlic cloves, finely chopped
3 tbsp chopped fresh parsley

pinch of freshly grated nutmeg
pinch of ground cloves
2 tbsp fresh white breadcrumbs
2 tbsp olive oil
salt and pepper

1. Preheat the oven to 200°C/400°F/Gas Mark 6. Mix the scallops, onions, garlic, 2 tablespoons of the parsley, the nutmeg and cloves together in a bowl and season to taste with salt and pepper.

2. Divide the mixture between four scrubbed scallop shells or heatproof dishes. Sprinkle the breadcrumbs and remaining parsley on top and drizzle with the oil.

3. Place in the preheated oven and bake for 15–20 minutes, or until lightly golden and piping hot. Serve immediately.

Tapenade

MAKES ABOUT 300 G/10½ OZ

250 g/9 oz black olives, such as Nyons
   or Niçoise, stoned

3 anchovy fillets in oil, drained

1 large garlic clove, halved, with the
   green centre removed if necessary

2 tbsp pine kernels

½ tbsp capers in brine, rinsed

125 ml/4 fl oz extra virgin olive oil

freshly squeezed lemon juice or orange
   juice, to taste

pepper

GARLIC CROÛTES

12 slices French bread, about
   5 mm/¼ inch thick

extra virgin olive oil, for brushing

2 garlic cloves, peeled and halved

1. Put the olives, anchovy fillets, garlic, pine kernels and capers in a food processor or blender and process until well blended. With the motor still running, pour the olive oil through the feed tube and continue blending until a loose paste forms.

2. Add the lemon juice and pepper to taste. Cover and chill until required.

3. To make the garlic croûtes, preheat the grill to high. Place the bread slices on the grill rack and toast 1 side for 1–2 minutes, or until golden brown. Flip the bread over, lightly brush the untoasted side with oil, then toast for 1–2 minutes.

4. Rub 1 side of each bread slice with the garlic cloves while it is still hot, then set aside and leave to cool completely. Store in an airtight container for up to 2 days.

5. Serve the tapenade with the garlic croûtes.

Hummus

SERVES 4

400 g/14 oz canned chickpeas

juice of 1 large lemon

6 tbsp tahini

2 tbsp olive oil

2 garlic cloves, crushed

salt and pepper

chopped fresh coriander and black
olives, to garnish

CIABATTA TOASTS

1 ciabatta loaf, sliced

2 garlic cloves, crushed

1 tbsp chopped fresh coriander

4 tbsp olive oil

1. To make the hummus, first drain the chickpeas, reserving a little of the liquid. Put the chickpeas and liquid in a food processor and blend, gradually adding the reserved liquid and lemon juice. Blend well after each addition until smooth.

2. Stir in the tahini and all but 1 teaspoon of the oil. Add the garlic, season to taste and blend again until smooth.

3. Spoon the hummus into a serving dish. Drizzle the remaining oil over the top and garnish with the chopped coriander and olives. Leave to chill in the refrigerator while preparing the ciabatta toasts.

4. Preheat the grill. Lay the slices of ciabatta on a grill rack in a single layer. Mix the garlic, coriander and oil together and drizzle over the bread slices. Cook under the preheated grill for 2–3 minutes until golden brown, turning once. Serve hot with the hummus.

Vegetables and Salads

Nurtured by the benign climate, vegetables hold pride of place throughout the Mediterranean region. It is, after all, one of the most fertile areas in the world, producing a bounty of fresh produce that has made the cuisine so famous. The importance of vegetables is evident in the countless dishes that start with an initial softening of chopped onions and garlic in olive oil, followed by tomatoes and other vegetables according to the dish. The process creates an all-important foundation of flavour, whether it is a pasta sauce, a Provençal stew, such as Ratatouille, or a Moroccan tagine.

Vegetables are often eaten on their own, either as a starter or as a separate course. They are generally served warm or at room temperature rather than piping hot. Some vegetables – fennel, for example – are eaten raw in salads; others, including French beans or broccoli, are lightly cooked and served with a

drizzle of olive oil or fresh lemon juice. Grilling and roasting is a popular method that really concentrates the flavours, bringing out the inherent sweetness of summer vegetables, or the meatiness of mushrooms and aubergines.

Salads range from classics such as Salade Niçoise and Caesar Salad to more substantial composed salads based on seafood or meat, or on grains, such as couscous or bulgar wheat.

The choice of greenery is enormous – peppery rocket, bitter-sweet chicory and endive, crisp lettuces and juicy purslane – a Middle-Eastern favourite. Soft leafy herbs, such as basil, coriander, mint and parsley, are used by the handful rather than as a garnish.

Patatas Bravas

SERVES 6

2 tbsp Spanish olive oil, plus extra
   for deep-frying

1 onion, finely chopped

2 garlic cloves, crushed

50 ml/2 fl oz white wine or dry Spanish
   sherry

400 g/14 oz canned chopped tomatoes

2 tsp white wine vinegar or
   red wine vinegar

1–2 tsp crushed dried chillies

2 tsp hot or sweet smoked Spanish
   paprika

1 kg/2 lb 4 oz potatoes

salt and pepper

1. Heat the oil in a saucepan, add the onion and cook over a medium heat, stirring
    occasionally, for 5 minutes, or until soft but not brown. Add the garlic and cook,
    stirring, for 30 seconds. Add the wine and bring to the boil. Add the tomatoes,
    vinegar, chillies and paprika, reduce the heat and simmer, uncovered, for
    10–15 minutes until a thick sauce forms.

2. When the sauce is cooked transfer it to a food processor or blender and process
    until smooth. Return the sauce to the pan and set aside.

3. Do not peel the potatoes, but cut them into chunky pieces. Heat enough oil in
    a large frying pan to come about 2.5 cm/1 inch up the sides of the pan. Add the
    potato pieces and cook over a medium–high heat, turning occasionally, for
    10–15 minutes until golden brown. Remove with a slotted spoon, drain on kitchen
    paper and sprinkle with salt to taste.

4. Meanwhile, gently reheat the sauce. Mix with the potatoes, transfer to a warmed
    serving dish and season with pepper. Serve the potatoes hot, with wooden cocktail
    sticks for spearing.

Greek Feta and Olive Tartlets

MAKES 12

butter, for greasing

plain flour, for dusting

175 g/6 oz ready-made shortcrust
   pastry

1 egg

3 egg yolks

300 ml/10 fl oz whipping cream

115 g/4 oz feta cheese (drained weight)

6 black Greek olives, stoned and halved

12 small fresh rosemary sprigs

salt and pepper

1. Preheat the oven to 200°C/400°F/Gas Mark 6. Grease 12 individual 6-cm/2½-inch tart tins, or the cups in a 12-hole muffin tin.

2. On a floured work surface, roll out the pastry to 3 mm/⅛ inch thick. Cut the pastry into rounds, use to line the prepared tins and prick the bases with a fork. Press a square of foil into each tartlet case and bake in the preheated oven for 12 minutes. Remove the foil and bake for a further 3 minutes.

3. Place the egg, egg yolks and cream in a bowl, add salt and pepper to taste and beat together.

4. Crumble the cheese into the tartlet cases and spoon over the egg mixture. Place half an olive and a rosemary sprig on top of each tartlet, then bake in the preheated oven for 15 minutes, or until the filling is just set.

5. Serve warm or cold.

Leek and Goat's Cheese Crêpes

MAKES 8

25 g/1 oz unsalted butter

½ tbsp sunflower oil

200 g/7 oz leeks, halved, rinsed and finely shredded

freshly grated nutmeg, to taste

1 tbsp finely snipped fresh chives

8 savoury crêpes

85 g/3 oz soft goat's cheese, rind removed if necessary, chopped

salt and pepper

1. Preheat the oven to 200°C/400°F/Gas Mark 6. Melt the butter with the oil in a heavy-based saucepan with a lid over a medium–high heat. Add the leeks and stir so that they are well coated. Add salt and pepper to taste and a few gratings of nutmeg, then cover the leeks with a sheet of wet greaseproof paper and cover the pan. Reduce the heat to very low and leave the leeks to sweat for 5–7 minutes until very tender, but not brown. Stir in the chives, then taste and adjust the seasoning if necessary.

2. Put 1 crêpe on the work surface and put one eighth of the leeks on the crêpe, top with one eighth of the cheese, then fold the crêpe into a square parcel or simply roll it around the filling. Place the stuffed crêpe on a baking tray, then continue to fill and fold or roll the remaining crêpes.

3. Put the crêpes in the preheated oven and bake for 5 minutes, or until they are hot and the cheese starts to melt. Serve hot.

Roast Summer Vegetables

SERVES 4

2 tbsp olive oil

1 fennel bulb

2 red onions

2 beef tomatoes

1 aubergine

2 courgettes

1 yellow pepper

1 red pepper

1 orange pepper

4 garlic cloves, peeled but left whole

4 fresh rosemary sprigs

pepper

crusty bread, to serve (optional)

1. Brush a large ovenproof dish with a little oil. Preheat the oven to 200°C/400°F/Gas Mark 6. Prepare the vegetables. Cut the fennel, onions and tomatoes into wedges. Thickly slice the aubergine and courgettes, then deseed the yellow pepper, red pepper and orange pepper and cut into chunks. Arrange the vegetables in the prepared dish and tuck the garlic cloves and rosemary sprigs among them. Drizzle with the remaining oil and season with pepper.

2. Roast the vegetables in the preheated oven for 10 minutes. Remove the dish from the oven and turn the vegetables over using a slotted spoon. Return to the oven and roast for a further 10–15 minutes, or until the vegetables are tender and starting to turn golden brown.

3. Serve the vegetables straight from the dish or transfer them to a warmed serving plate. Serve with crusty bread, if using.

Ratatouille

SERVES 4

3 red peppers

200 ml/7 fl oz olive oil

250 g/9 oz courgettes, thickly sliced

1 fennel bulb, roughly chopped

2 large red onions, roughly sliced

3 white onions, thickly sliced

2 large aubergines, thickly sliced

600 g/1 lb 5 oz ripe tomatoes, peeled and deseeded

1 large tbsp fresh thyme leaves

1 large tbsp fresh rosemary leaves

1 tsp sugar

salt and pepper

1. Preheat the grill to high, then put the red peppers on the grill tray and grill until the skin blackens. Turn and grill again, continuing until they are blackened all over. Put them in a bowl and cover with clingfilm to sweat for 10 minutes, then peel them under cold running water. Cut them open and deseed them, then chop the flesh into large chunks.

2. Meanwhile, place a large heavy-based saucepan over a medium heat and add half the oil. Add the courgettes and fry until they begin to brown. Transfer them to a large roasting tin and keep warm. Add the fennel and onions to the pan and fry for 15–20 minutes until they soften, then transfer them to the roasting tin. Add the aubergines and some more oil (they will soak up a lot) and fry until they begin to brown. Add them to the roasting tin, laid flat in a single layer.

3. Preheat the oven to 190°C/375°F/Gas Mark 5. Add the tomatoes, red peppers, thyme and rosemary to the roasting tin and distribute the vegetables evenly across it in a single layer. Sprinkle the sugar over and gently mix through. If you need more room, use two roasting tins. Season with salt and pepper and drizzle with the remaining oil, then place, uncovered, in the preheated oven and cook for 40–50 minutes until the vegetables start to brown. Serve hot.

Risotto with Asparagus and Walnuts

SERVES 4

15 g/½ oz butter

3 tbsp olive oil

1 small onion, finely chopped

350 g/12 oz risotto rice

150 ml/5 fl oz dry white wine

1.5 litres/2¾ pints hot vegetable stock

200 g/7 oz asparagus tips,
   cut into 6-cm/2½-inch lengths

40 g/1½ oz chopped walnuts

grated rind of 1 lemon

salt and pepper

walnut oil, to serve (optional)

strips of lemon zest, to garnish

1. Heat the butter and oil in a large saucepan, add the onion and fry, stirring, for 3–4 minutes until soft.

2. Add the rice and stir over a medium heat for 1 minute, without browning.

3. Add the wine and boil rapidly, stirring, until it has almost evaporated.

4. Stir the stock into the pan a ladleful at a time, allowing each ladleful to be absorbed before adding more.

5. After 10 minutes, add the asparagus tips and continue cooking, adding stock when necessary.

6. After a further 5 minutes, test a grain of rice – it should be tender, but still firm to the bite.

7. Stir in the walnuts and lemon rind, then adjust the seasoning, adding salt and pepper to taste. Remove from the heat and drizzle over a little walnut oil, if using, stirring in lightly. Garnish with strips of lemon zest and serve.

Vegetable Tagine

SERVES 4

2–3 tbsp olive oil or argan oil

2 onions, halved and sliced with the grain

4 garlic cloves, chopped

25 g/1 oz fresh ginger, peeled and chopped

1–2 red chillies, deseeded and chopped

1 tsp cumin seeds

1 tsp paprika

2 potatoes, peeled and thickly sliced

2 carrots, peeled and thickly sliced

600 ml/1 pint vegetable stock or chicken stock

225 g/8 oz fresh shelled peas or frozen peas

1 bunch of fresh coriander, roughly chopped

3–4 tomatoes, sliced

15 g/½ oz butter

salt and pepper

Summer Couscous Salad (see page 72), to serve

1. Heat the oil in a tagine or heavy-based, flameproof casserole, add the onions and cook over a medium heat, stirring frequently, for 2–3 minutes until they begin to colour. Add the garlic, ginger and chillies and cook, stirring, for 1–2 minutes. Stir in the cumin seeds and paprika, then toss in the potatoes and carrots. Pour in the stock and bring to the boil. Reduce the heat, cover and simmer for 10 minutes, or until the potatoes and carrots are tender but still firm. Season to taste with salt and pepper. Preheat the oven to 200°C/400°F/Gas Mark 6 if using a tagine, or 180°C/350°F/Gas Mark 4 if using a casserole.

2. Toss in the peas and half the coriander. Arrange the tomato slices over the top and dot with the butter. Transfer, uncovered, to the oven and bake for 10 minutes, if using a tagine, or 15 minutes, if using a casserole, until the tomatoes are brown on top.

3. Garnish with the remaining coriander and serve hot with Summer Couscous Salad.

Fettuccine with Garlic, Tomatoes and Olives

SERVES 4

4 plum tomatoes, peeled, deseeded and chopped

4 garlic cloves, finely chopped

8 black olives, stoned and finely chopped

1 fresh red chilli, deseeded and finely chopped

2 tbsp chopped fresh flat-leaf parsley, plus extra to garnish

2 tbsp extra virgin olive oil

1 tbsp lemon juice

280 g/10 oz dried fettuccine

salt and pepper

1. Place the tomatoes in a large, non-metallic sieve set over a bowl. Cover and set aside in the refrigerator for 30 minutes.

2. Combine the garlic, olives, chilli, parsley, oil and lemon juice in a separate bowl. Season to taste with salt and pepper. Cover and set aside in the refrigerator until required.

3. Add the tomatoes to the garlic mixture, discarding the drained juice.

4. Bring a large saucepan of lightly salted water to the boil. Add the fettuccine, return to the boil and cook for 8–10 minutes, or until tender but still firm to the bite. Drain, then tip into a serving bowl. Add the garlic and tomato mixture and toss well. Garnish with chopped parsley and serve immediately.

Traditional Greek Salad

SERVES 4

200 g/7 oz Greek feta cheese

½ head Webbs lettuce or 1 lettuce such as cos or escarole, shredded or sliced

4 tomatoes, cut into quarters

½ cucumber, sliced

12 black Greek olives, stoned

2 tbsp chopped fresh herbs, such as oregano, flat-leaf parsley, mint or basil, to garnish

DRESSING

6 tbsp extra virgin olive oil

2 tbsp fresh lemon juice

1 garlic clove, crushed

pinch of sugar

salt and pepper

1. To make the dressing, put all the ingredients into a small screw-top jar and shake until well blended. Set aside. Cut the cheese into cubes about 2.5 cm/1 inch square. Put the lettuce, tomatoes and cucumber in a salad bowl. Scatter over the cheese and toss together.

2. Just before serving, whisk the dressing, pour over the salad leaves and toss together. Scatter over the olives and chopped herbs and serve.

Tabbouleh

SERVES 4

175 g/6 oz quinoa

600 ml/1 pint water

10 vine-ripened cherry tomatoes, halved

7.5-cm/3-inch piece cucumber, diced

3 spring onions, finely chopped

juice of ½ lemon

2 tbsp extra virgin olive oil

4 tbsp chopped fresh mint

4 tbsp chopped fresh coriander

4 tbsp chopped fresh parsley

salt and pepper

1. Put the quinoa into a medium-sized saucepan and cover with the water. Bring to the boil, then reduce the heat, cover and simmer over a low heat for 15 minutes. Drain if necessary.

2. Leave the quinoa to cool slightly before combining with the remaining ingredients in a salad bowl. Adjust the seasoning to taste before serving.

Summer Couscous Salad

SERVES 4

350 g/12 oz couscous

½ tsp salt

400 ml/14 fl oz warm water

1–2 tbsp olive oil

4 spring onions, finely chopped
 or sliced

1 bunch of fresh mint, finely chopped

1 bunch of fresh flat-leaf parsley, finely
 chopped

1 bunch of fresh coriander, finely
 chopped

15 g/½ oz butter

½ preserved lemon, finely chopped

1. Preheat the oven to 180°C/350°F/Gas Mark 4. Tip the couscous into an ovenproof
    dish. Stir the salt into the water and then pour over the couscous. Cover and leave
    the couscous to absorb the water for 10 minutes.

2. Drizzle the oil over the couscous. Using your fingers, rub the oil into the grains to
    break up the lumps and aerate them. Toss in the spring onions and half the herbs.
    Dot the surface with the butter and cover with a piece of foil or wet greaseproof
    paper. Bake in the preheated oven for about 15 minutes to heat through.

3. Fluff up the grains with a fork and tip the couscous into a warmed serving dish.
    Toss the remaining herbs into the couscous and scatter the preserved lemon over
    the top. Serve hot with grilled meats, fish or vegetable dishes.

Pastrami and Pepper Antipasti Salad

SERVES 4

1 Webbs lettuce
280 g/10 oz chargrilled pepper
    antipasti in oil
115 g/4 oz sunblush tomatoes in oil
115 g/4 oz green olives, stoned
115 g/4 oz wafer-thin pastrami
fresh basil leaves, to garnish

DRESSING
2 tbsp balsamic vinegar
1 tsp Dijon mustard
pinch of sugar
salt and pepper

1. Tear the lettuce into small chunks and place in a serving bowl. Drain the pepper antipasti and the tomatoes, reserving 4 tablespoons of the oil. Roughly chop the peppers and tomatoes and toss into the lettuce with the olives.

2. To make the dressing, put the reserved oil and the rest of the dressing ingredients into a small screw-top jar and shake until well blended. Pour half the dressing over the salad and toss well to mix. Arrange the pastrami in ruffles on top of the salad. Serve drizzled with the rest of the dressing and garnished with basil leaves.

Ham and Salami Salad With Figs

SERVES 6

9–12 ripe figs, depending on size

6 thin slices dry-cured Italian ham

12 thin slices salami

1 small bunch of fresh basil, separated into small sprigs

few fresh mint sprigs

1 small bunch of rocket leaves

2 tbsp freshly-squeezed lemon juice

4 tbsp extra virgin olive oil

salt and pepper

1. Trim the fig stems to leave just a short length, then cut the figs into quarters.

2. Arrange the ham and salami on a large serving platter.

3. Wash and dry the herbs and rocket and put in a bowl with the prepared figs.

4. Whisk the lemon juice and oil together with a fork in a small bowl and season well with salt and pepper. Pour over the herbs and salad leaves and carefully turn the figs and leaves in the dressing until they are well coated.

5. Spoon the figs and salad onto the meat and serve.

Lamb Kofte Salad

SERVES 4

400 g/14 oz lean minced lamb

1 small onion, finely chopped

2 tsp ground coriander

2 tsp ground cumin

2 tsp paprika

1 tbsp chopped fresh coriander

2 tbsp chopped fresh mint

3 tbsp olive oil

115 g/4 oz mixed baby leaf and herb
   salad

1 tbsp lemon juice

salt and pepper

CUCUMBER AND MINT YOGURT

6 tbsp natural yogurt

85 g/3 oz cucumber, grated

2 tsp mint sauce

salt and pepper

1. Place 12 wooden skewers in a shallow bowl of cold water and leave to soak for 30 minutes. Place the lamb, onion, spices and the fresh coriander and mint into a food processor or blender and season with salt and pepper. Process for 1–2 minutes until finely minced. Transfer to a bowl, cover and chill in the refrigerator for 30 minutes.

2. Preheat the grill to medium–high. Divide the lamb mixture into 12 and wrap around the soaked wooden skewers to form oval shapes. Brush with a little of the oil and grill the skewers under the preheated grill for 15–20 minutes, turning frequently until cooked through.

3. To make the cucumber and mint yogurt mix together the yogurt, cucumber and mint sauce in a small bowl and season with salt and pepper.

4. Place the salad leaves in a large bowl. Whisk together the remaining oil with the lemon juice and season to taste. Pour over the salad leaves and toss until coated. Serve the hot koftes, on or off the skewers, with the salad and the cucumber and mint yogurt.

Salade Niçoise

SERVES 4

2 tuna steaks, about 2 cm/¾ inch thick

olive oil, for brushing

250 g/9 oz French beans, topped and
  tailed

125 ml/4 fl oz vinaigrette or garlic
  vinaigrette dressing

2 hearts of lettuce, leaves separated

3 large hard-boiled eggs, quartered

2 juicy vine-ripened tomatoes,
  cut into wedges

50 g/1¾ oz anchovy fillets in oil,
  drained

55 g/2 oz Niçoise olives, stoned

salt and pepper

1. Heat a ridged cast-iron griddle pan over a high heat until you can feel the heat
   rising from the surface. Brush the tuna steaks with oil, then place, oiled side down,
   on the hot pan and chargrill for 2 minutes. Lightly brush the top side of the tuna
   steaks with more oil. Use a pair of tongs to turn the steaks over, then season to
   taste with salt and pepper. Continue chargrilling for a further 2 minutes for rare or
   for up to 4 minutes for well done. Leave to cool.

2. Meanwhile, bring a saucepan of lightly salted water to the boil. Add the beans,
   return to the boil, then boil for 3 minutes, or until tender-crisp. Drain the beans
   and immediately transfer them to a large bowl. Pour over the vinaigrette and stir
   together, then leave the beans to cool in the dressing.

3. To serve, transfer the lettuce leaves to a dish. Lift the beans out of the bowl,
   leaving the excess behind, and put them in the dish with the lettuce. Break the
   tuna into large pieces and arrange over the beans. Arrange the eggs and tomatoes
   around the side. Place the anchovy fillets on top of the salad, then scatter with the
   olives. Drizzle the remaining dressing in the bowl over everything and serve.

Caesar Salad

SERVES 4

1 large egg

2 cos lettuces or 3 Little Gem lettuces

6 tbsp olive oil

2 tbsp lemon juice

8 canned anchovy fillets, drained and roughly chopped

85 g/3 oz fresh Parmesan cheese shavings, to garnish

salt and pepper

GARLIC CROÛTONS

4 tbsp olive oil

2 garlic cloves

5 slices white bread, crusts removed, cut into 1-cm/½-inch cubes

1. Bring a small, heavy-based saucepan of water to the boil.

2. Meanwhile, make the garlic croûtons. Heat the oil in a heavy-based frying pan. Add the garlic and diced bread and cook, stirring and tossing frequently, for 4–5 minutes, or until the bread is crispy and golden all over. Remove from the pan with a slotted spoon and drain on kitchen paper.

3. While the bread is frying, add the egg to the boiling water and cook for 1 minute, then remove from the saucepan and reserve.

4. Arrange the lettuce leaves in a salad bowl. Mix the oil and lemon juice together, then season to taste with salt and pepper. Crack the egg into the dressing and whisk to blend. Pour the dressing over the lettuce leaves, toss well, then add the croûtons and anchovies and toss the salad again. Sprinkle with Parmesan cheese shavings and serve.

Mixed Seafood Salad

SERVES 4–6

2 garlic cloves, crushed

juice of 1½ lemons

4 tbsp extra virgin olive oil

2 tbsp chopped fresh flat-leaf parsley

600 g/1 lb 5 oz cooked seafood cocktail (prawns, mussels, clams, calamari rings, cockles)

1 oil-cured roasted red pepper, sliced into thin strips

12 stoned black olives

2 tbsp shredded fresh basil

salt and pepper

1. Whisk the garlic, lemon juice, oil and parsley with salt and pepper to taste.

2. Drain the seafood if necessary, and tip into a serving dish. Add the red pepper and olives, then mix with the garlic mixture, turning to coat. Leave in a cool place for 30 minutes to allow the flavours to develop.

3. Stir again before serving, check the seasoning and sprinkle with the basil.

Meat and Poultry

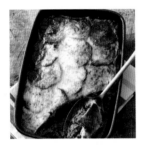  

The rocky terrain and dry soil of much of the Mediterranean area mean that available grazing is limited, and meat is therefore not such an important feature of the cuisine as it is elsewhere in the world. Beef, when it does appear on the menu, is more often slowly braised in wine to tenderize tough but tasty cuts.

In general, sheep and pigs do far better in the Mediterranean environment than cattle, as is evident from the number of dishes in which they appear. Moussaka, claimed by the Greeks as their national dish, is made with lamb, as are Lebanese 'kibbeh' and the well-known Turkish döner kebab. Pork is popular in Greece and in central Italy where it is sold roasted, with crisp and juicy crackling, in the many open-air markets. Spit-roasting and grilling over coals or scented wood embers

are the preferred methods of cooking; sausages and offal, juicy chops and kebabs, and whole pigs and sheep are all cooked in this way. Complicated sauces are unheard of, and flavouring is usually a sprinkling of herbs and lemon juice, a dribble of olive oil and a few turns of the pepper mill.

All types of poultry are eaten, from the ubiquitous chicken to turkey, duck and small birds, such as pigeon and quail. Chicken shows up in countless dishes – plainly roasted or grilled, simmered in flavoursome stews, stuffed with nuts and rice, and also in 'bestilla', a magnificent cinnamon-scented pie baked in Morocco for special occasions. Leftovers are always put to good use in soups, pasta sauces and risotto.

Lasagne al Forno

SERVES 4

2 tbsp olive oil

55 g/2 oz pancetta, chopped

1 onion, chopped

1 garlic clove, finely chopped

225 g/8 oz fresh minced beef

2 celery sticks, chopped

2 carrots, chopped

pinch of sugar

½ tsp dried oregano

400 g/14 oz canned chopped tomatoes

2 tsp Dijon mustard

140 g/5 oz Cheddar cheese, grated

300 ml/10 fl oz ready-made Béchamel sauce

225 g/8 oz no pre-cook lasagne sheets

115 g/4 oz freshly grated Parmesan cheese, plus extra for sprinkling

salt and pepper

1. Preheat the oven to 190°C/375°F/Gas Mark 5. Heat the oil in a large, heavy-based saucepan. Add the pancetta and cook over a medium heat, stirring occasionally, for 3 minutes, or until the fat begins to run. Add the onion and garlic and cook, stirring occasionally, for 5 minutes, or until soft.

2. Add the beef and cook, breaking it up with a wooden spoon, until brown all over. Stir in the celery and carrots and cook for 5 minutes. Season to taste with salt and pepper. Add the sugar, oregano and tomatoes and their can juices. Bring to the boil, reduce the heat and simmer for 30 minutes.

3. Meanwhile, stir the mustard and Cheddar cheese into the Béchamel sauce.

4. In a large, rectangular ovenproof dish, make alternate layers of meat sauce, lasagne sheets and Parmesan cheese. Pour the cheese sauce over the layers, covering them completely, and sprinkle with Parmesan cheese. Bake in the preheated oven for 30 minutes, or until golden brown and bubbling. Serve the lasagne immediately.

Ultimate Spaghetti Bolognese

SERVES 8

4 tbsp olive oil, plus extra
  to toss with the pasta

500 g/1 lb 2 oz minced beef

500 g/1 lb 2 oz sausage meat,
  peeled Italian sausages or
  chopped pork belly

6 garlic cloves, chopped

250 ml/9 fl oz red wine

400 g/14 oz canned chopped plum
  tomatoes

800 g/1 lb 12 oz red peppers,
  deseeded and roughly chopped

2 red chillies, chopped

100 ml/3½ fl oz white wine vinegar

small handful of chopped oregano

large handful of chopped parsley

800 g/1 lb 12 oz dried spaghetti

salt and pepper

grated Parmesan cheese and a green
  salad, to serve

1. Heat a wide, heavy-based saucepan or casserole dish over a medium heat, add half the oil and the beef and sausage meat. Break up with a wooden spoon and fry until it starts to brown, stirring occasionally. After about 20 minutes add the garlic and cook for a further 5 minutes. Spoon off any excess and add the wine and tomatoes. Stir and reduce the heat to a very gentle simmer.

2. Heat the remaining oil in another wide saucepan, add the peppers and fry, stirring occasionally, for about 20 minutes until they start to brown. Add the chillies and vinegar and cook for a further 5 minutes.

3. Add the peppers and the oregano to the meat mixture, and season to taste with salt and pepper. Cover loosely and leave to simmer very gently for 30 minutes. If the mixture looks like drying out, add some more wine. Add the parsley a couple of minutes before serving.

4. Cook the pasta according to the instructions on the packet. Drain, return to the saucepan and toss with a little olive oil. Mix the meat mixture with the pasta and serve with some grated Parmesan cheese and a green salad.

Beef Braised in Red Wine

SERVES 6

3 tbsp olive oil

2 onions, finely sliced

2 garlic cloves, chopped

1 kg/2 lb 4 oz stewing steak, cut into thick strips

2 tbsp plain flour

300 ml/10 fl oz good-quality red wine, such as Chianti

2 fresh sage leaves

200 ml/7 fl oz beef stock or vegetable stock

1 tbsp tomato purée

salt and pepper

1 tbsp finely chopped fresh flat-leaf parsley, to garnish

1. Preheat the oven to 150°C/300°F/Gas Mark 2. Heat 1 tablespoon of the oil in a large frying pan, add the onions and garlic and cook over a medium heat, stirring frequently, for 6–8 minutes until soft and brown. Remove with a slotted spoon and transfer to a casserole.

2. Heat the remaining oil in the pan, add the steak strips and cook over a high heat, stirring, for 3–4 minutes until brown all over. Sprinkle in the flour and stir well to prevent lumps forming. Season well with salt and pepper. Reduce the heat to medium, pour in the wine, stirring constantly, and bring to the boil, continuing to stir constantly.

3. Carefully turn the contents of the pan into the casserole. Add the sage, stock and tomato purée, cover and cook in the centre of the preheated oven for 2½–3 hours.

4. Remove from the oven, discard the sage and taste and adjust the seasoning if necessary. Serve immediately, scattered with the parsley.

Sausage Pizza

SERVES 2–4

2 tbsp olive oil, plus extra for brushing

1 ready-made 25-cm/10-inch pizza base

200 g/7 oz chorizo or other spicy sausages

55 g/2 oz freshly grated Parmesan cheese

400 g/14 oz canned chopped tomatoes

115 g/4 oz pancetta or bacon, cut into thin slices

1 tbsp fresh basil leaves

1. Preheat the oven to 200°C/400°F/Gas Mark 6. Brush a baking sheet with oil. Place the pizza base on the baking sheet and push up the edge a little.

2. Remove and discard the sausage casings and crumble the meat into a bowl. Add the cheese and mix well.

3. Spoon the tomatoes evenly over the pizza base almost to the edge, then sprinkle with the sausage mixture. Top with the pancetta and basil leaves, and drizzle with the olive oil. Bake for 20 minutes until the edge of the pizza base is crisp and golden. Serve immediately.

Quiche Lorraine

SERVES 4

15 g/½ oz butter

1 small onion, finely chopped

4 lean streaky bacon rashers, diced

55 g/2 oz Gruyère cheese or Cheddar
  cheese, grated

2 eggs, beaten

300 ml/10 fl oz single cream

pepper

PASTRY

200 g/7 oz plain flour, plus extra
  for dusting

100 g/3½ oz salted butter

1–2 tbsp cold water

1. For the pastry, sift the flour into a bowl and rub in the butter with your fingertips
    until the mixture resembles fine breadcrumbs. Stir in just enough water to bind
    the mixture to a firm dough. Roll out the dough on a lightly floured work surface
    to a round slightly larger than a 23-cm/9-inch loose-based round tart tin, 3 cm/1¼
    inches deep. Lift the pastry onto the tin and press it down into the fluted edge,
    using the back of your finger. Roll the rolling pin over the edge of the tin to trim off
    the excess pastry. Prick the base all over with a fork and chill in the refrigerator for
    at least 10 minutes to allow the pastry to rest and prevent shrinkage.

2. Preheat the oven to 200°C/400°C/Gas Mark 6 and preheat a baking tray. Place a
    sheet of baking paper in the pastry-lined tin. Fill with baking beans, place on the
    baking tray and bake in the preheated oven for 10 minutes. Remove the paper and
    beans and bake for a further 10 minutes.

3. Melt the butter in a frying pan and cook the onion and bacon over a medium
    heat for about 5 minutes, stirring occasionally, until the onion is soft and lightly
    browned. Spread the mixture evenly in the hot pastry case and sprinkle with half
    the cheese. Beat together the eggs and cream in a small bowl and season with
    pepper. Pour into the pastry case and sprinkle with the remaining cheese. Reduce
    the oven temperature to 190°C/375°F/Gas Mark 5. Place the quiche in the oven
    and bake for 25–30 minutes, or until golden brown and just set. Leave to cool for
    10 minutes before turning out.

Tartiflette

SERVES 4

1 kg/2 lb 4 oz small waxy potatoes, sliced

2 tbsp olive oil

3 garlic cloves, peeled but kept whole

150 g/5½ oz bacon lardons

600 ml/1 pint double cream

2 tbsp fresh thyme leaves

200 g/7 oz Reblochon cheese or any other good melting cheese, sliced

salt and pepper

1. Preheat the oven to 180°C/350°F/Gas Mark 4.

2. Bring a large saucepan of lightly salted water to the boil, add the potato slices and cook for 10–15 minutes until just tender. Drain.

3. Heat the oil in a large frying pan over a medium heat. Hit the garlic cloves with the back of a sturdy knife to split them and add them to the frying pan. Add the bacon lardons and fry for 3–4 minutes until just cooked. Add the potato slices and cook for 3–4 minutes. Pour in the cream, add the thyme leaves and stir well.

4. Transfer the mixture to a gratin dish and top with the cheese slices. Bake in the preheated oven for 20 minutes, or until golden and bubbling.

Catalan Sausage and Bean Stew

SERVES 6

2 tbsp olive oil, plus extra for frying

5 rashers unsmoked bacon, derinded
    and cut into 1-cm/½-inch strips

2 onions, chopped

3 large garlic cloves, finely chopped

6 large pork sausages

450 g/1 lb chorizo sausage, in 1 piece

400 g/14 oz canned butter beans,
    drained and rinsed

1 litre/1¾ pints chicken stock

250 g/9 oz fresh or frozen broad beans

6 tbsp chopped flat-leaf parsley

crusty bread, to serve

1. Heat the oil in a casserole and fry the bacon over a medium–low heat for
    10 minutes until starting to colour. Remove with a slotted spoon and set aside.
    Add the onions and gently fry for 15 minutes, stirring, until golden. Add the garlic
    and fry for a further 5 minutes.

2. Meanwhile, put the pork sausages in a frying pan and cook over a medium heat,
    in a little oil if necessary, and without pricking them, until golden but not brown.
    Remove from the pan and slice each sausage into four pieces. Remove the skin
    from the chorizo, and slice into 2.5-cm/1-inch chunks.

3. Return the bacon to the casserole, then add both types of sausage and the butter
    beans. Pour in the stock, cover and bring to the boil, then reduce the heat and
    simmer for 15 minutes.

4. Add the broad beans and half the parsley. Return to the boil, then simmer for
    5 minutes until just tender (do not overcook). Sprinkle with the remaining parsley
    and serve with hunks of crusty bread to mop up the juices.

Provençal Lamb with Garlic and Herbs

SERVES 4

1.5 kg/3 lb 5 oz stewing lamb, cubed

3 tbsp olive oil

10–15 garlic cloves, peeled

1 tbsp chopped mixed herbs, such as rosemary, thyme, oregano or marjoram

water or stock

125 ml/4 fl oz dry white wine

salt and pepper

fresh rosemary sprigs, to garnish

1. Sprinkle the meat with a little salt. Heat the oil in a heavy-based casserole. Add the meat and gently fry over a medium–high heat, in batches if necessary, until brown.

2. Add the garlic, cover tightly and cook over a very low heat, stirring occasionally, for 1 hour, or until most of the liquid has evaporated and the meat is beginning to sizzle in its own fat.

3. Add the herbs and continue to cook for 30–40 minutes, or until the meat is very tender, adding a spoonful of water from time to time, so that there is always a little liquid in the base of the casserole.

4. Transfer the meat to a plate using a slotted spoon. Pour off the fat from the casserole. Stir in the wine and cook for a few minutes, scraping with a wooden spoon to dissolve any sediment in the base of the casserole.

5. Return the meat to the casserole and simmer for a few minutes, turning to coat with the sauce. Season with plenty of pepper, and more salt if necessary. Garnish with rosemary sprigs just before serving.

Moussaka

SERVES 4

2 aubergines, thinly sliced

450 g/1 lb lean minced beef or lamb

2 onions, thinly sliced

1 tsp finely chopped garlic

400 g/14 oz canned tomatoes

2 tbsp chopped fresh parsley

2 eggs

300 ml/10 fl oz Greek-style yogurt

1 tbsp freshly grated Parmesan cheese

salt and pepper

1. Dry-fry the aubergine slices, in batches, in a non-stick frying pan on both sides until brown. Remove from the pan.

2. Add the beef to the frying pan and cook for 5 minutes, stirring, until brown. Stir in the onions and garlic and cook for a further 5 minutes, or until brown. Add the tomatoes, parsley, and salt and pepper, then bring to the boil and simmer for 20 minutes, or until the meat is tender.

3. Preheat the oven to 180°C/350°F/Gas Mark 4. Arrange one third of the aubergine slices in a layer in an ovenproof dish. Add half the meat mixture, then half the remaining aubergine slices. Add the remaining meat mixture and layer the remaining aubergine slices on top.

4. Beat the eggs in a bowl, then beat in the yogurt and add salt and pepper to taste. Pour the mixture over the aubergines and sprinkle the grated cheese on top.

5. Bake the moussaka in the preheated oven for 45 minutes, or until golden brown. Serve straight from the dish.

Lamb Tagine with Sticky Dates and Olives

SERVES 8

1.5–2 kg/3 lb 5 oz–4 lb 8 oz boned lamb shoulder, trimmed of fat and chopped into 4-cm/1½-inch cubes

4 tbsp olive oil

250 g/9 oz stoned dates

250 g/9 oz stoned olives

700 ml/1¼ pints red wine

10 whole garlic cloves, peeled

large handful of fresh coriander

cooked couscous mixed with lemon zest and thyme leaves, to serve

DRY MARINADE

2 large Spanish onions, grated

4 garlic cloves, crushed

1 red chilli, deseeded and finely chopped

1 tsp paprika

2 tsp ground cumin

1 tsp ground ginger

1 tsp pepper

1. Combine all the dry marinade ingredients in a casserole, add the lamb and leave to marinate in the refrigerator for 4 hours or overnight.

2. Preheat the oven to 150°C/300°F/Gas Mark 2. Remove the lamb from the refrigerator. Add the oil, dates, olives, wine and garlic to the casserole and cover. Transfer to the preheated oven and cook for 2½ hours, removing the lid for the last 30 minutes. Check that the lamb is meltingly tender, stir in the coriander and serve with couscous.

Classic Chicken Pie with Cinnamon

SERVES 4–6

2–3 tbsp olive oil

100 g/3½ oz butter

3 onions, halved lengthways, then halved crossways and sliced with the grain

2 garlic cloves, chopped

2–3 tbsp blanched almonds, chopped

1–2 tsp ground cinnamon, plus extra for dusting

1 tsp ground ginger

1 tsp paprika

1 tsp ground coriander

250 g/9 oz chicken fillets, cut into bite-sized pieces

1 bunch of fresh flat-leaf parsley, finely chopped

1 large bunch of fresh coriander, finely chopped

7–8 sheets filo pastry, thawed if frozen

1 egg yolk, mixed with 1 tsp water

salt and pepper

1. Preheat the oven to 200°C/400°F/Gas Mark 6. Heat the oil in a heavy-based frying pan with a knob of the butter, add the onions and cook over a medium heat, stirring frequently, for 2–3 minutes, or until they begin to soften and colour.

2. Stir in the garlic and almonds and cook for 2 minutes, stirring, until the almonds begin to colour, then add the spices. Add the chicken and cook gently for 3–4 minutes, or until all the liquid in the pan has evaporated. Add the herbs, season to taste with salt and pepper and leave to cool.

3. Melt the remaining butter in a small saucepan. Separate the sheets of pastry and keep covered with a clean, damp tea towel. Brush a little melted butter over the base of a round ovenproof dish and cover with a sheet of pastry, allowing the sides to flop over the edge. Brush the pastry with melted butter and place another sheet on top. Repeat with another two layers.

4. Spread the chicken and onion mixture on top of the pastry and fold the edges over the filling. Cover with the remaining sheets of pastry, brushing each one with butter. Tuck the overlapping edges under the pie or arrange them attractively on top of the pie. Brush the egg yolk mixture over the top of the pie to glaze. Bake in the preheated oven for 25 minutes, or until the pastry is puffed up and golden. Dust the top with cinnamon and serve immediately.

Chicken, Mushroom and Cashew Nut Risotto

SERVES 4

55 g/2 oz butter

1 onion, chopped

250 g/9 oz skinless, boneless chicken breasts, diced

350 g/12 oz risotto rice

1 tsp ground turmeric

350 ml/12 fl oz white wine

1.3 litres/2¼ pints simmering chicken stock

75 g/2¾ oz chestnut mushrooms, sliced

50 g/1¼ oz cashew nuts, halved

salt and pepper

TO GARNISH

wild rocket

fresh Parmesan cheese shavings

fresh basil leaves

1. Melt the butter in a large saucepan over a medium heat. Add the onion and cook, stirring occasionally, for 5 minutes, or until soft. Add the chicken and cook, stirring frequently, for a further 5 minutes. Reduce the heat, add the rice and mix to coat in butter. Cook, stirring constantly, for 2–3 minutes, or until the grains are translucent. Stir in the turmeric, then add the wine. Cook, stirring constantly, for 1 minute until reduced.

2. Gradually add the stock, a ladleful at a time. Stir constantly and add more liquid as the rice absorbs each addition. Increase the heat to medium so that the liquid bubbles. Cook for 20 minutes, or until all the liquid is absorbed and the rice is creamy. About 3 minutes before the end of the cooking time, stir in the mushrooms and cashew nuts. Season to taste with salt and pepper.

3. Remove the risotto from the heat and spoon into individual serving dishes. Sprinkle over the rocket, Parmesan cheese shavings and basil leaves and serve.

Fettuccine with Chicken and Basil Pesto

SERVES 4

2 tbsp vegetable oil

4 skinless, boneless chicken breasts

350 g/12 oz dried fettuccine

salt and pepper

sprig of fresh basil,
   to garnish

PESTO

100 g/3½ oz shredded fresh basil

125 ml/4 fl oz extra virgin olive oil

3 tbsp pine kernels

3 garlic cloves, crushed

55 g/2 oz freshly grated Parmesan
   cheese

2 tbsp freshly grated pecorino cheese

salt

1. To make the pesto, put the basil, oil, pine kernels, garlic and a generous pinch of salt into a food processor or blender. Process the ingredients until smooth. Scrape the mixture into a bowl and stir in the Parmesan cheese and pecorino cheese.

2. Heat the oil in a frying pan over a medium heat. Add the chicken breasts and cook, turning once, for 8–10 minutes until the juices are no longer pink. Cut into small cubes.

3. Meanwhile, bring a large saucepan of lightly salted water to the boil. Add the pasta, return to the boil and cook for 8–10 minutes, or until tender but still firm to the bite. Drain and transfer to a warmed serving dish. Add the chicken and pesto, then season to taste with pepper. Toss well to mix.

4. Garnish with a sprig of basil and serve warm.

Rolled Turkey Escalopes With Parma Ham and Sage

SERVES 4

6 turkey steaks, weighing about
   150 g/5½ oz each

150 g/5½ oz Parma ham, very
   thinly sliced

12 sage leaves

flour, for dusting

2 tbsp vegetable oil

25 g/1 oz butter

300 ml/10 fl oz white wine

200 g/7 oz canned chopped tomatoes

pinch of sugar

salt and pepper

small sage sprigs, to garnish

cooked French beans, to serve

1. Slice the turkey steaks in half crossways to make 12 pieces. Place each piece between two sheets of clingfilm and pound until very thin. Try to make the pieces roughly rectangular in shape, about 13 x 9 cm/5 x 3½ inches, trimming the edges if necessary. Place a slice of ham on top, followed by a sage leaf. Fold up the narrow ends to meet in the middle, then fold in half again. Secure with a wooden cocktail stick inserted lengthways so that the parcels will sit flat in the pan. Dust all over with flour.

2. Heat a large frying pan over a medium–high heat and add the oil and two thirds of the butter. Add the turkey parcels and fry for 7–8 minutes, turning, until golden. Transfer to a warmed plate and remove the cocktail sticks. Season to taste with salt and pepper.

3. Pour the wine into the pan and simmer briskly for 2 minutes, scraping up any sediment from the base of the pan. Add the tomatoes, bring to the boil and simmer for 3 minutes, stirring. Swirl in the remaining butter, and season with a pinch of sugar and salt and pepper.

4. Return the turkey to the pan with any juices, and simmer until heated through, turning to coat with the sauce. Tip into a warmed serving dish and garnish with sage sprigs. Serve with French beans.

Classic Roasted Duck Breast with Sweet Redcurrant Sauce

SERVES 4

4 duck breasts, skin on
½ tbsp vegetable oil
4 shallots, finely chopped
2 garlic cloves, crushed
2 tbsp fresh thyme leaves
200 ml/7 fl oz red wine

4 tbsp sherry or balsamic vinegar
85 g/3 oz redcurrant jelly
55 g/2 oz butter, cut into chunks
salt and pepper
glazed carrots, to serve

1. Preheat the oven to 180°C/350°F/Gas Mark 4. Score the skin of each duck breast with four diagonal cuts down to the fat (but not into the meat). Season with salt and pepper. Place a large, heavy-based frying pan over a high heat, add the oil and then the duck breasts, skin side down. Sear for about 10 minutes until the skin is crisp. Turn the breasts over and sear on the other side for 2 minutes. Remove from the frying pan and put into a roasting tin. Keep warm.

2. Pour off most of the fat from the pan, reserving about 1 tablespoon. Place the pan over a medium heat, add the shallots and fry for 5–10 minutes until soft. Meanwhile, put the duck breasts into the preheated oven and cook for about 15 minutes. Add the garlic and thyme to the pan and cook for a further 2 minutes. Add the wine and vinegar, simmer for 5 minutes, then stir in the redcurrant jelly and butter. When the duck is cooked, remove it from the oven, cover and keep warm for 5 minutes.

3. Cut each breast diagonally into five fat slices, lay on warmed plates and pour over the sauce. Serve with roast potatoes, watercress salad and glazed carrots.

Breads and Desserts

In Mediterranean countries a meal without bread is unheard of – it appears without fail at the table to nibble on while you wait for the meal to begin. Types of breads vary from country to country and region to region. There are the rough rustic loaves of France and Italy, with their crackly crusts and chewy interiors – indispensable for mopping up juices and the last of a soup, and for filling with gutsy ingredients, including salami, roasted peppers and cheese. Soft spongy focaccia, flavoured with onion and rosemary, is immensely popular throughout Italy and is eaten at all times of the day. Then there are irresistible 'morning' breads, as they are known in the trade, Croissants and Biscotti – indispensable with a steaming cup of coffee to kick-start the day.

In the Middle East, unleavened flatbread is perfect for scooping up creamy hummus and tahini. Cut in half, the pocket makes a perfect receptacle for falafel and salad.

Desserts are often simple affairs, especially in the Middle East where they usually consist of a bowl of seasonal fruit, a freshly made fruit salad or a cooked fruit compôte. Sweet pastries such as Baklava are popular for serving on special occasions. Creamy chilled desserts, such as Panna Cotta and Crème Brûlée, are perennial favourites in Italy and France. The Spanish national dessert is 'Flan' – a baked custard made with eggs, sugar and milk, sometimes flavoured with oranges or rum.

Stromboli with Salami, Roasted Peppers and Cheese

MAKES 1 LOAF

500 g/1 lb 2 oz strong white flour, sifted

1¾ tsp easy-blend dried yeast

2 tsp sea salt flakes

3 tbsp olive oil, plus extra for brushing

350 ml/12 fl oz lukewarm water

FILLING

85 g/3 oz thinly sliced Italian salami

175 g/6 oz mozzarella cheese, chopped

25 g/1 oz basil leaves

2 red peppers, roasted, peeled, deseeded and sliced

pepper

1. Mix the flour, yeast and 1½ tsp salt in a bowl, then stir in the oil with enough water to make a soft dough. Turn out onto a lightly floured work surface and knead for about 10 minutes. Cover and leave in a warm place for 1 hour, or until doubled in volume. Turn out onto a floured work surface again and lightly knead for 2–3 minutes until smooth. Cover and set aside for a further 10 minutes.

2. Turn out the dough onto a floured work surface and roll out to a rectangle measuring about 38 x 25 cm/15 x 10 inches, 1 cm/½ inch thick.

3. Preheat the oven to 200°C/400°F/Gas Mark 6. Spread the salami over the dough and top with the mozzarella cheese, basil and red peppers. Season with pepper.

4. Grease a baking sheet. Firmly roll up the dough from the long side, pinch the ends and place on the baking sheet, join underneath. Cover and set aside for 10 minutes.

5. Pierce the roll deeply several times with a skewer. Brush with oil and sprinkle with the remaining salt. Bake in the preheated oven for 30–35 minutes, or until firm and golden. Remove from the oven and leave to cool on a wire rack.

Chorizo Bread Parcels

MAKES 16

200 g/7 oz strong white flour,
  plus extra for dusting

1½ tsp easy-blend dried yeast

½ tsp salt

¼ tsp caster sugar

125 ml/4 fl oz warm water

sunflower oil, for oiling

115 g/4 oz chorizo sausage,
  outer casing removed

1. Put the flour, yeast, salt and sugar into a large bowl and make a well in the centre. Pour the water into the well and gradually mix in the flour from the side. Using your hands, mix together to form a soft dough that leaves the side of the bowl clean.

2. Turn out the dough onto a lightly floured work surface and knead for 10 minutes, or until smooth and elastic and no longer sticky. Shape the dough into a ball and put in a clean bowl. Cover with a clean, damp tea towel and leave in a warm place for 1 hour, or until the dough has risen and doubled in size.

3. Preheat the oven to 200°C/400°F/Gas Mark 6. Oil a baking sheet. Cut the chorizo sausage into 16 equal-sized chunks. Turn out the risen dough onto a lightly floured work surface and knead lightly for 2–3 minutes to knock out the air. Divide into 16 equal-sized pieces. Shape each piece into a ball and roll out on a lightly floured work surface to a 12-cm/4½-inch round. Put a piece of chorizo on each round, gather the dough at the top, enclosing the chorizo, and pinch the edges together to seal. Put each parcel, pinched-side down, on the prepared baking sheet.

4. Bake in the preheated oven for 20 minutes until pale golden brown. Turn the parcels over so that the pinched ends are uppermost and arrange in a serving basket. Serve hot, as soon after baking as possible.

Turkish Flatbread

MAKES 8

750 g/1 lb 10 oz plain flour, plus extra
   for dusting
1½ tsp salt
1 tsp ground cumin
½ tsp ground coriander

1 tsp caster sugar
1 sachet easy-blend dried yeast
2 tbsp olive oil, plus extra for brushing
400 ml/14 fl oz lukewarm water

1. Sift the flour, salt, cumin and coriander together into a bowl and stir in the sugar
   and yeast. Make a well in the centre and pour in the olive oil and water. Stir well
   with a wooden spoon until the dough begins to come together, then knead with
   your hands until it leaves the side of the bowl. Turn out onto a lightly floured work
   surface and knead well for about 10 minutes until smooth and elastic.

2. Brush a bowl with oil. Shape the dough into a ball, put it in the bowl and put the
   bowl into a polythene bag or cover with a damp tea towel. Leave to rise in a warm
   place for 1 hour until the dough has doubled in volume.

3. Lightly brush a baking sheet with oil. Turn out the dough onto a lightly floured work
   surface, knock back with your fist and knead for 1–2 minutes. Divide the dough into
   eight equal pieces, shape each piece into a ball, then roll out to a 20-cm/8-inch
   round. Cover the rounds with a damp tea towel and leave to rest for 20 minutes.

4. Heat a heavy-based frying pan and brush the base with oil. Add 1 dough round,
   cover and cook for 2–3 minutes until lightly browned on the underside. Turn over
   with a fish slice, re-cover the pan and cook for a further 2 minutes until lightly
   browned on the second side. Remove from the pan and cook the remaining dough
   rounds in the same way.

Olive and Sun-dried Tomato Bread

MAKES 2 LOAVES

400 g/14 oz plain flour, plus extra
for dusting

1 tsp salt

1 sachet easy-blend dried yeast

1 tsp brown sugar

1 tbsp chopped fresh thyme

200 ml/7 fl oz lukewarm water

4 tbsp olive oil, plus extra for brushing

55 g/2 oz black olives, stoned and
sliced

55 g/2 oz green olives, stoned and
sliced

100 g/3½ oz sun-dried tomatoes in oil,
drained and sliced

1 egg yolk, beaten

1. Sift the flour and salt together into a bowl and stir in the yeast, sugar and thyme. Make a well in the centre and pour in the water and oil. Stir well with a wooden spoon until the dough begins to come together, then knead with your hands until it leaves the side of the bowl. Turn out onto a lightly floured surface and knead in the olives and tomatoes, then knead for a further 5 minutes until the dough is smooth and elastic.

2. Brush a bowl with oil. Shape the dough into a ball, put it in the bowl and put the bowl into a polythene bag or cover with a damp tea towel. Leave to rise in a warm place for 1–1½ hours until the dough has doubled in volume.

3. Dust a baking sheet with flour. Turn out the dough onto a lightly floured work surface and knock back with your fist. Cut it in half and, with lightly floured hands, shape each half into a round or oval. Put on the prepared baking sheet and put the baking sheet into a polythene bag or cover with a damp tea towel. Leave to rise in a warm place for 45 minutes.

4. Preheat the oven to 200°C/400°F/Gas Mark 6. Make 3 shallow diagonal slashes on the top of each loaf and brush with the beaten egg yolk. Bake for 40 minutes until golden brown and the loaves sound hollow when tapped on the base with your knuckles. Transfer to a wire rack to cool.

Almond Biscotti

MAKES 20–30

200 g/7 oz whole blanched almonds

200 g/7 oz plain flour, plus 1 tbsp
 for dusting

200 g/7 oz caster sugar, plus 1 tbsp
 for sprinkling

1 tsp baking powder

½ tsp ground cinnamon

2 eggs

2 tsp vanilla extract

1. Preheat the oven to 180°C/350°F/Gas Mark 4. Line two baking sheets with baking paper. Chop the almonds very coarsely, leaving some whole.

2. Mix the flour, sugar, baking powder and cinnamon together in a mixing bowl. Stir in all the almonds.

3. Beat the eggs with the vanilla extract in a small bowl, then add to the flour mixture and mix together to form a firm dough.

4. Turn out the dough onto a lightly floured work surface and knead lightly. Divide in half and shape each piece into a long, thick log, roughly 5 cm/2 inches wide.

5. Transfer to the prepared baking sheets and sprinkle with sugar, then bake in the preheated oven for 20–25 minutes, or until brown and firm. Remove from the oven and leave to cool for a few minutes, then transfer the logs to a chopping board and cut into 1-cm/½-inch slices.

6. Meanwhile, reduce the oven temperature to 160°C/325°F/Gas Mark 3. Arrange the biscuits, cut-side down, on the baking sheets. Bake in the oven for 15–20 minutes, or until dry and crisp. Remove from the oven and leave to cool on a wire rack. Store in an airtight container to keep crisp.

Italian Chocolate Chip Bread

MAKES 1 LOAF

vegetable oil, for brushing

225 g/8 oz plain flour, plus extra
for dusting

1 tbsp cocoa powder

pinch of salt

15 g/½ oz butter, plus ½ tsp melted
butter for brushing

1 tbsp caster sugar

1 sachet easy-blend dried yeast

150 ml/5 fl oz lukewarm water

55 g/2 oz plain chocolate chips

1. Brush a baking sheet with oil. Sift the flour, cocoa powder and salt together into a bowl. Add the butter and cut it into the dry ingredients, then stir in the sugar and yeast. Gradually add the water, stirring well with a wooden spoon until the dough begins to come together, then knead with your hands until it leaves the side of the bowl. Turn out onto a lightly floured work surface and knead for about 10 minutes until smooth and elastic.

2. Knead the chocolate chips into the dough, then form into a round loaf. Put the loaf on the prepared baking sheet and put the baking sheet into a polythene bag or cover with a damp tea towel. Leave to rise in a warm place for 1–1½ hours until the dough has doubled in volume.

3. Preheat the oven to 220°C/425°F/Gas Mark 7. Bake the loaf for 10 minutes, then reduce the oven temperature to 190°C/375°F/Gas Mark 5 and bake for a further 15 minutes.

4. Transfer the loaf to a wire rack and brush the top with the melted butter. Cover with a tea towel and leave to cool.

Croissants

MAKES 6

500 g/1 lb 2 oz strong white flour, sifted, plus extra for dusting

40 g/1½ oz caster sugar

1 tsp salt

2 tsp easy-blend dried yeast

300 ml/10 fl oz lukewarm milk

300 g/10½ oz butter, softened, plus extra for greasing

1 egg, lightly beaten with 1 tbsp milk, for glazing

1. Preheat the oven to 200°C/400°F/Gas Mark 6. Mix the dry ingredients in a large bowl, make a well in the centre and add the milk. Mix to a soft dough, adding more milk if too dry. Knead on a lightly floured work surface for 5–10 minutes, or until smooth and elastic. Place in a large greased bowl, cover and leave in a warm place until doubled in volume.

2. Meanwhile, place the butter between two sheets of baking paper. Flatten with a rolling pin to form a 5 mm/¼ inch thick rectangle. Place in the refrigerator until required.

3. Knead the dough for 1 minute, then turn out onto a well-floured work surface and roll out to 45 x 15 cm/18 x 6 inches. Place the butter in the centre of the dough, fold up the sides and squeeze the edges together gently. With the short end of the dough towards you, fold the top third down and the bottom third up. Give it a quarter turn, roll out as big as the original rectangle and fold again. If the butter feels soft, wrap the dough in clingfilm and chill. Repeat the rolling process twice more.

4. Cut the dough in half and roll out each half into a 5-mm/¼-inch thick rectangle. Use a cardboard triangular template, base 18 cm/7 inches and sides 20 cm/8 inches, to cut out the croissants. Brush the triangles with the egg and milk mixture. Roll into croissant shapes, tucking the point underneath. Brush again with the glaze. Place on a baking sheet and leave to double in volume. Bake in the preheated oven for 15–20 minutes until golden brown.

Quick Tiramisù

SERVES 4

225 g/8 oz mascarpone cheese
   or soft cheese
1 egg, separated
2 tbsp natural yogurt
2 tbsp caster sugar

2 tbsp dark rum
2 tbsp cold strong black coffee
8 sponge fingers
2 tbsp grated plain chocolate

1. Put the mascarpone cheese, egg yolk and yogurt in a large bowl and beat together until smooth.

2. Whip the egg white in a separate, grease-free bowl until stiff but not dry, then beat in the sugar and gently fold into the cheese mixture. Divide half the mixture between four sundae glasses.

3. Mix the rum and coffee together in a shallow dish. Dip the sponge fingers into the rum mixture, break them in half, or into smaller pieces if necessary, and divide between the glasses.

4. Stir any remaining coffee mixture into the remaining cheese mixture and divide between the glasses.

5. Sprinkle with the grated chocolate. Serve immediately or cover and chill in the refrigerator until required.

Crème Brûlée

SERVES 8

500 ml/18 fl oz double cream
1 vanilla pod
100 g/3½ oz caster sugar, plus extra
   for the topping
6 egg yolks

1. Preheat the oven to 160°C/325°F/Gas Mark 3.

2. Pour the cream into a small saucepan. Split the vanilla pod in half lengthways,
   scrape the seeds into the pan, then chop the pod into little pieces and add to the
   pan. Heat the cream to boiling point, then reduce the heat and leave to simmer
   gently for 5 minutes.

3. Put the sugar and egg yolks in a heatproof bowl and beat with a spoon until well
   mixed. Pour the hot cream into the egg mixture, beating (not whisking) as you
   pour, until nicely thickened. Pass through a fine sieve into another bowl or jug.
   Pour the mixture into eight small shallow dishes and lay in a roasting tray. Boil a
   kettle and carefully pour the hot water into the tray so that it comes halfway up the
   sides of the crème brûlée dishes.

4. Place in the preheated oven and bake for about 35–45 minutes until the custard
   has just set.

5. Remove from the oven and leave to cool to room temperature. Sprinkle some
   caster sugar over the custard and then gently caramelize it using a kitchen blow
   torch, or under a very hot grill. Leave to cool for a few minutes, then serve.

Baklava

MAKES 9

150 g/5½ oz shelled pistachio nuts, finely chopped

75 g/2¾ oz toasted hazelnuts, finely chopped

75 g/2¾ oz blanched hazelnuts, finely chopped

grated rind of 1 lemon

1 tbsp brown sugar

1 tsp ground mixed spice

150 g/5½ oz butter, melted, plus extra for greasing

250 g/9 oz (about 16 sheets) frozen filo pastry, thawed

250 ml/9 fl oz water

2 tbsp clear honey

1 tbsp lemon juice

300 g/10½ oz caster sugar

½ tsp ground cinnamon

1. Preheat the oven to 160°C/325°F/Gas Mark 3. Place the nuts, lemon rind, brown sugar and mixed spice in a bowl and mix well. Grease a 20 x 20-cm/8 x 8-inch square cake tin with butter. Cut the whole stack of filo pastry sheets to the size of the tin. Keep the filo sheets covered with a damp tea towel.

2. Lay a pastry sheet on the base of the tin and brush with melted butter. Add another six sheets of pastry on top, brushing between each layer with melted butter. Spread over one third of the nut mixture, then add three sheets of buttered pastry. Spread over another third of nut mixture then top with three more sheets of buttered pastry. Spread over the remaining nut mixture and add the last three sheets of buttered pastry. Cut into squares, then bake in the oven for 1 hour.

3. Meanwhile, place the water, honey, lemon juice, caster sugar and cinnamon in a saucepan. Bring to the boil, stirring. Reduce the heat and simmer, without stirring, for 15 minutes. Leave to cool. Remove the baklava from the oven, pour over the syrup and leave to set before serving.

Spanish Flan

SERVES 4–6

500 ml/18 fl oz milk

½ orange with 2 long, thin pieces of rind removed

1 vanilla pod, split, or ½ tsp vanilla extract

175 g/6 oz caster sugar

4 tbsp water

butter, for greasing

3 large eggs

2 large egg yolks

1. Pour the milk into a saucepan with the orange rind and vanilla pod. Bring to the boil, remove from the heat and stir in 100 g/3½ oz of the sugar; set aside for at least 30 minutes to infuse.

2. Meanwhile, put the remaining sugar and the water in another saucepan over a medium–high heat. Stir until the sugar dissolves, then boil without stirring until the caramel turns a deep golden brown. Immediately remove the saucepan from the heat and add some orange juice to stop the cooking. Pour into a lightly buttered 1.2-litre/2-pint soufflé dish and swirl to cover the base; set aside.

3. When the milk has infused, return the saucepan to the heat, add the milk and bring to a simmer. Beat the eggs and egg yolks together in a heatproof bowl. Pour the warm milk into the eggs, whisking constantly. Strain into the soufflé dish.

4. Meanwhile, preheat the oven to 160°C/325°F/Gas Mark 3. Place the soufflé dish in a roasting tin and pour in enough boiling water to come halfway up the sides of the dish. Bake in the preheated oven for 75–90 minutes until set and a knife inserted in the centre comes out clean.

5. Remove the soufflé dish from the roasting tin and set aside to cool completely. Cover and chill overnight. To serve, run a metal spatula around the side of the dish, then invert onto a serving plate with a rim, shaking firmly to release.

Panna Cotta

SERVES 4

1 vanilla pod
475 ml/16 fl oz double cream
4½ tbsp sugar

4 sheets clear gelatine
500 g/1 lb 2 oz strawberries
3 tbsp icing sugar

1. Cut the vanilla pod lengthways and scrape out the seeds. Pour the cream into a saucepan, add the vanilla pod and seeds and bring to the boil over a medium heat. Stir in the sugar and simmer over a low heat for 15 minutes.

2. Soak the gelatine in cold water for about 10 minutes, then drain or press the liquid from the gelatine. Pour the hot cream through a sieve into a bowl, then dissolve the gelatine in it.

3. Rinse four small soufflé dishes in cold water and fill with the cream. Chill overnight in the refrigerator. Wash the strawberries, setting aside a few for decoration. Cook the remaining strawberries with the icing sugar. While hot, press the berries through a sieve into a bowl and then leave to cool.

4. To serve, turn out the soufflé dishes onto dessert plates, top with strawberry sauce and decorate with the reserved whole berries.

Honey and Lemon Tart

SERVES 8–12

375 g/13 oz cottage cheese, cream
   cheese or ricotta cheese

6 tbsp Greek honey

3 eggs, beaten

½ tsp cinnamon

grated rind and juice of 1 lemon

PASTRY

225 g/8 oz plain flour

pinch of salt

1½ tsp caster sugar

150 g/5½ oz butter, diced

3–4 tbsp cold water

1. To make the pastry, put the flour, salt, sugar and butter into a food processor. Mix in short bursts until the mixture resembles fine breadcrumbs. Sprinkle over the water and mix until a smooth dough forms. Alternatively, make the pastry in a bowl and rub in with your hands. The pastry can be used straight away but is better if allowed to rest in the refrigerator, wrapped in greaseproof paper or foil, for about 30 minutes before use.

2. If using cottage cheese for the filling, push the cheese through a sieve into a bowl. Add the honey to the cheese and beat until smooth. Add the eggs, cinnamon, lemon rind and lemon juice, and mix well together.

3. Preheat the oven to 200°C/400°F/Gas Mark 6. Roll out the pastry on a lightly floured surface and use to line a 23-cm/9-inch tart tin. Place on a baking sheet and line with greaseproof paper. Weigh down with baking beans and bake in the preheated oven for 15 minutes. Remove the greaseproof paper and beans and bake for a further 5 minutes until the base is firm but not brown.

4. Reduce the oven temperature to 180°C/350°F/Gas Mark 4. Pour the filling into the pastry case and bake in the oven for about 30 minutes until set. Serve cold.

Crêpes Suzette

SERVES 4

8 sweet crêpes
2 tbsp brandy

ORANGE SAUCE
55 g/2 oz caster sugar
1 tbsp water
finely grated rind of 1 large orange

125 ml/4 fl oz freshly squeezed
    orange juice
55 g/2 oz unsalted butter, diced
1 tbsp Cointreau, Grand Marnier or
    other orange-flavoured liqueur

1. To make the orange sauce, place the sugar in a wide sauté pan or frying pan over a
    medium heat and stir in the water. Continue stirring until the sugar dissolves, then
    increase the heat to high and leave the syrup to bubble for 1–2 minutes until it just
    begins to turn golden brown.

2. Stir in the orange rind and juice, then add the butter and continue stirring until it
    melts. Stir in the liqueur.

3. Lay one of the crêpes flat in the sauté pan and spoon the sauce over. Using a fork
    and the spoon, fold the crêpe into quarters and push to the side of the pan. Add
    the next crêpe to the pan and repeat. Continue until all the crêpes are coated with
    the sauce and folded. Remove the pan from the heat.

4. Warm the brandy in a ladle or small saucepan, ignite and pour it over the crêpes to
    flambé, shaking the sauté pan.

5. When the flames die down, serve the crêpes with the sauce spooned over.

Pistachio Ice Cream with Grilled Mango Slices

SERVES 4–6

1 ripe mango, stoned,
  peeled and sliced

icing sugar, for sprinkling

ICE CREAM

175 g/6 oz blanched pistachio nuts,
  finely ground

300 ml/10 fl oz milk

300 ml/10 fl oz double cream

4 egg yolks

175 g/6 oz granulated sugar

2–3 tbsp rosewater or orange flower
  water

1. To make the ice cream, put the nuts, reserving about 2 teaspoons for decorating, in a heavy-based saucepan with the milk and cream and bring to the boil over a medium heat.

2. In a large bowl, beat the egg yolks with the sugar, then pour in the hot milk and cream, beating constantly. Pour the custard mixture back into the saucepan and cook over a low heat, stirring constantly, until it thickens, and turn off the heat. Stir in the rosewater and leave the mixture to cool. Pour into a freezerproof container and freeze for 1 hour, or until partially frozen. Remove from the freezer, transfer to a bowl and beat to break down the crystals. Freeze again for 30 minutes, then beat again. Freeze once more until firm. Alternatively, churn in an ice cream maker, following the manufacturer's instructions.

3. Remove the ice cream from the freezer and leave to stand for 10–15 minutes before serving. Meanwhile, preheat the grill to high. Sprinkle the mango slices with icing sugar and grill for 3–4 minutes, or until they are slightly caramelized. Serve immediately with scoops of the ice cream, decorated with a sprinkling of the reserved ground pistachio nuts.

Index